Attention

My dreams are found in this journal.
In case of loss, please return to:

_____
_____
_____
_____

Note From Creator

Dear Friend,

Every day is a gift. Work to honor each one you are given. Through regular writing, pondering, visualization and thought work, you will have opportunities to create many wonderful moments in your life.

I hope this journal helps you find a pathway to personal fulfillment and realized dreams along the way. The thought downloads, models, and self-coaching ninja routine, if applied and used, have the potential to be life changing.

Life is a beautiful combination of freedom mixed with struggle; light mixed with dark; new mixed with old; and love mixed with heartache. Both sides are essential to the human experience. Open up to it all, embrace it all, and experience what it feels like to live an unstoppable life.

Your dreams should scare you, or they just aren't big enough.

X,

Amy Twiggs
Mental Strength Coach

Copyright

ISBN-13: 978-1-949015-10-2

Orientation

Dear Friend,

Before you begin making your dreams a reality, spend some time creating a clear picture of what you truly want and why. This will increase your motivation on days when obstacles seem to be growing and energy seems to be waning. Have a clear vision first, create your dream second.

This book has been set up for you to do regular thought downloads and self-coaching models as taught in the Flippin' Awesome Coaching Program. Prompts and activities are also included to help you uncover beliefs that may be limiting you. If you need help with these tools, you are welcome to get answers at FlippinAwesomeCoaching.com.

Your Thoughts Downloads and Unintentional Models will show what you are currently creating in your life and why.

Once you are aware of your own Unintentional Models, use the Intentional Model space to purposefully choose a different thought, feeling, action, and result. Sometimes we just want to see what is happening, why it's happening, and then we still choose to keep everything the same. There is no right or wrong, good or bad in these thought downloads or models. They are for information and optional transformation. Use the Intentional Model to achieve your dreams.

The workbook ends with journal space to dream about what is possible for you, why you might want to reach for future goals, and record any inspiration along the way.

If your vision is clear, you are committed to your goal and consistent in your effort, then there is nothing you can't achieve.

YOU GOT THIS!

▼ Questions to Consider ◀

To help clarify your vision when doing Intentional Models

Questions to ask regarding any current thought or limiting beliefs:

1. What if you believed you were 100% amazing?
2. Without any limiting thoughts, who would you be?
3. Is your current thought serving your future dream?
4. Why are you choosing to think that thought?
5. What result is that thought producing for you?
6. What if the thought you're focused on right now isn't true?
7. Can you come up with evidence that the opposite is true?
8. Would you be willing to give that thought up?
9. Do you see that belief in other areas of your life?
10. What are you making that thought mean about you?
11. Do you really believe that thought is true?
12. Are there other ways to think about your circumstance that might feel better and get you closer to your dream?
13. What will believing that thought cost you in your sport?
14. Let's say that thought is true. Now what?
15. Even if that thought is true, is it helping you achieve your goal?
16. Have you had enough of that thought?
17. How is everything happening *for you* in your life right now?
18. How is the "worst thing" also the "best thing?"
19. How can you make today more fun?
20. What if nothing has gone wrong?
21. What can you learn from your current situation that you didn't know before?
22. Who is the person you've become because that happened?
23. What if you are exactly where you are supposed to be?
24. What if you already knew the answer to all your questions?
25. What can you do right now to get the result you want?
26. If you weren't afraid to fail, what else would you do?
27. If you were certain that you would succeed either way, what decision would you make?
28. What would your goals look like if they were **easy**?
29. How much of your sport are you missing out on by believing your current thought?
30. What if you didn't have to be comfortable to take action?

Questions to Consider

Questions to do ask during difficult times

1. How is happening for you?
2. How is this an opportunity for you?
3. How do you want to show up in this situation?
4. What if you were right where you wanted to be?
5. What if nothing has gone wrong?
6. What's funny about this?
7. Are you making room for grief?
8. What did you learn from this that you didn't know before?
9. Who is the person you have become because this happened?
10. What if you are exactly where you're supposed to be?

Questions to ask every day

1. How can you be an example of what's possible?
2. How can you get your stuff done and have fun at the same time?
3. What can you do to laugh a lot today?
4. How can you make today better than yesterday?
5. How can you make your future more exciting than your past?
6. How can you make yourself a priority so you have more to give to others?
7. What do you love about yourself?
8. What are you grateful for?
9. How can you honor your body today?
10. How can you feel more connected to your internal joy?
11. How can you make choices that benefit you and everyone around you at the same time?
12. How can you live your best life?

Possibilities

WHAT DO YOU BELIEVE IS POSSIBLE FOR YOU? WHY?
Room For You To Dream

Obstacles & Strategies

There are obstacles with any dream. On the lines below, pick ONE dream, then list every obstacle you can imagine, knowing you will not be able to foresee them all. Next to each obstacle write at least one pre-planned strategy you will use to get through the inherent obstacle.

DREAM: _____

_____Obstacles:_____   _____Strategies:_____

Self-Coaching Model

How Solve Any Problem & Create Any Dream

The self-coaching model (CTFAR) is the foundational tool that I teach clients in order to clearly identify the CAUSE to any struggle. It's also the formula used to generate future dreams. This self-coaching model was created by my mentor and Master Coach Brooke Castillo.

When you don't know why you are getting a result in your sport or life, there is a simple step by step solution. You do a thought download, pick a thought from that download, put the thought in a model, then ask questions to fill in the rest of the model (these questions are provided on the following pages). Completing these steps will show you why you are getting your current results.

The model you produce is called an "*Unintentional Model.*" An *Unintentional Model* means you may not have been consciously aware of a thought that is creating your current result.

To change a current result (or to make any dream come true), you work through what we call an "*Intentional Model.*" With *Intentional Models,* you keep the circumstance the same from the *Unintentional Model*, **choose** a result you intentionally want to experience, then work backwards up the model to create a focused pathway to get that result for yourself.

With an *Intentional Model*, you can also pre-decide how you want **any** model component to be (Thoughts, Feelings, Actions, or Results) and fill in the model based around that one component change without changing the circumstance.

The amazing truth of the model is that you never have to change a circumstance in order to design a completely different result for yourself.

A description and examples of the 5 self-coaching ninja model components are included on the following page.

Self-Coaching Ninja Routine Instructions

Here are the instructions for the Self-Coaching Ninja Routine using the self-coaching model (CTFAR) as taught in the Flippin' Awesome Coaching Program:

- Step 1: Do a "Thought Download." A "Thought Download" (or TDL) is essentially where you write without stopping, without thinking, without judging, and as a way to find out what is going on in your lower or subconscious brain. Don't think about what you want to write, just write.

- Step 2: Pick one thought/sentence from your "TDL" and re-write it in the Unintentional Model at the T-line (Thought). The Unintentional Model will show you what you are creating in your life. Complete the Unintentional Model by asking yourself:
  - What is this thought regarding? (this will give you the C-line or Circumstance)
  - When I think this thought about the Circumstance, how do I Feel? (write one word in the F-line (Feeling)).
  - When I Feel this way, what action or inaction do I take? Put everything you do or don't do in the A-line (Action).
  - And when I do ALL of these Actions, what Result do I get in my life? Your answer goes in the R-line (Result).
  - Then, check your Result. Result is always proof of your Thought.

- Step 3: Using the same C-line content from the Unintentional Model, complete an Intentional Model. In this model, you can intentionally decide what Thought you want to think, what Feeling you want to feel, what Actions you want to take, and what Result you want to have. You can start anywhere, or at any line, on the model. You can put ANYTHING you want in the Intentional Model Result Line and create the formula for success by working backwards up the model.

Remember: Anything is possible for you. Keep practicing. Notice how you create your own results by your thoughts, feelings, and actions at all times.

The 5 Model Components

A Description & Examples of the 5 Model Components: **CTFAR**

1. *C*ircumstance (C-line): Facts, neutral, objective, no emotions attached, everyone would agree with you, outside of your control

    i.e. people, people's words, people's actions, places, your past, things, temperature outside, your age, the sport you play, the scoreboard, number on a scale, job, hair color, height, sibling count, nationality

2. *T*hought (T-line): A sentence on your brain, drama, meaning you give to any given circumstance, story you choose about your circumstance, subjective, descriptive, your personal power of choice, your agency, the CAUSE of all of your problems and results, always in your control

    i.e. "That person is rude.", "The weather is cold.", "I am too busy.", "I'm afraid I will disappoint.", "I am worried.", "My coach makes me mad.", "I have a lot of confidence.", "Work Is hard.", "I am an amazing person.", "I am afraid to fail."

3. *F*eelings (F-line): Vibrations. One word. Feelings are chemicals released by your brain when you focus on a Thought. The chemicals move or "vibrate" in your body. Your body was made to process these chemicals (neurotransmitters/hormones). In the model, we write what vibrations we feel when we focus on a single thought.

    i.e. Happy, Sad, Angry, Anxious, Stressed, Excited...

4. *A*ctions (A-line): Action, Inaction, Reaction. Anything you do or don't do because of a Feeling.

    i.e. Listen to a coach, hesitate, balk, gossip, spin in thoughts of doubt, learn a new skill, create something, quit, make no decisions, complain, show up

5. *R*esults (R-line): The effect of all your Actions, your overall life experience, the outcome. This is always proof of your original Thought.

    i.e. Realized Dreams, Championship Wins, Completed Projects, Accomplished Goals, Increased Confidence

Self-Coaching Ninja Model (CTFAR) Example Page

► CTFAR MODEL ◄

HOW TO SOLVE ANY PROBLEM

C= *CIRCUMSTANCE:* Facts, neutral, out of your control, no opinion, no emotion

↓ **TRIGGER**

T=*THOUGHTS:* Sentences, meaning we give to circumstances/life, optional, drama, our stories, about 50,000/day. Choose one to question.

↓ **GENERATE**

F=*FEELINGS:* Vibrations, one word description. What thought is creating this emotion?

↓ **FUEL**

A=*ACTIONS:* Action/Inaction/Reaction. When you feel this way, what do you do or not do?

↓ **CREATE**

R=*RESULT:* Effect of your actions. Evidence for your thought

When you want to feel better or create a specific result, use this model to see what you are creating and how you can choose a new thought to fulfill your dreams.

Unintentional Model

C: _____

_____

T: _____

_____

F: _____

_____

A: _____

_____

R: _____

_____

Intentional Model

C: _____

_____

T: _____

_____

F: _____

_____

A: _____

_____

R: _____

_____

Thought Download (TDL) Instructions

A thought download (tdl), free write, or brain dump are terms that simply imply that you are not consciously deciding what you want to write on the page. Instead of planning, dreaming, or deciding what to write, you just write until you are ready to stop or set a timer.

The only rule is that you can't stop writing until the timer goes off. Even if you don't know what else to write then just write, "I don't know what else to write at this time."

Repeat that phrase until something else pours out on the page. This practice will be crucial to find out what is happening in your default or lower brain.

This is different from journaling. When you journal, you are very aware of what you are writing and thinking. Journaling requires focus and conscious decisions. When you free write, your mind isn't focused on future goals or intentional thoughts.

If you want to see what is holding you back from your dreams, what limiting beliefs you may not be aware of or why you aren't taking the action you know is possible for you, then do a thought download regularly on any given topic.

The sentences that you write may surprise you at times. Don't judge them, just be curious and compassionate with yourself. We all have beliefs based on our evolution, our upbringing, our past experience, our biology and our culture.

None of your thoughts are problems unless you make them mean something that doesn't serve you. Just let your mind open up as you do thought downloads. Think of thought downloads like a regular cleaning out of your brain.

Letter From Future Self

Write a letter from your Future Self, who's right where you want to be, and have her/him give you some advice. What would she/he tell you to stop doing? What would he/she tell you to start doing? What else might she/he say?

CONTRACT WITH MYSELF

I hereby commit to giving this journal my all. I commit to work hard, take action & be accountable to my future self.

By signing below, I am making a commitment to continue believing in myself and work towards achieving my future realized goals even when I don't feel like taking action.

I understand that If I work hard & follow through with my Intentional Models, I WILL be successful. I will achieve impossible dreams while learning many new capabilities along the way.

Impossible Goal: _____

_____

Signature:_____
Today's Date: _____
Accomplished Goal Date: _____

CONGRATULATIONS!

If you have read and understood the instructions for Thought Downloads, Models, and the Self-Coaching Ninja Routine, then you are ready to take some massive action towards your goals!

Consistency is key for the remainder of this journal. You don't have to be extreme, just consistent.

You are stronger than you think you are.

Everything you do is a choice.

YOU GOT THIS!

Thought Download

Unintentional Model

C: _____
_____

T: _____
_____

F: _____
_____

A: _____
_____

R: _____
_____

Intentional Model

C: _____
_____

T: _____
_____

F: _____
_____

A: _____
_____

R: _____
_____

Thought Download

Unintentional Model

C: _____
_____

T: _____
_____

F: _____
_____

A: _____
_____

R: _____
_____

Intentional Model

C: _____
_____

T: _____
_____

F: _____
_____

A: _____
_____

R: _____
_____

Thought Download

Unintentional Model

C: _____
_____

T: _____
_____

F: _____
_____

A: _____
_____

R: _____
_____

Intentional Model

C: _____
_____

T: _____
_____

F: _____
_____

A: _____
_____

R: _____
_____

Thought Download

Unintentional Model

C: _____
_____

T: _____
_____

F: _____
_____

A: _____
_____

R: _____
_____

Intentional Model

C: _____
_____

T: _____
_____

F: _____
_____

A: _____
_____

R: _____
_____

►Thought Download◄

Unintentional Model

C: _____
_____

T: _____
_____

F: _____
_____

A: _____
_____

R: _____
_____

Intentional Model

C: _____
_____

T: _____
_____

F: _____
_____

A: _____
_____

R: _____
_____

Thought Download

Unintentional Model

C: _____
_____

T: _____
_____

F: _____
_____

A: _____
_____

R: _____
_____

Intentional Model

C: _____
_____

T: _____
_____

F: _____
_____

A: _____
_____

R: _____
_____

Thought Download

Unintentional Model

C: _____
_____

T: _____
_____

F: _____
_____

A: _____
_____

R: _____
_____

Intentional Model

C: _____
_____

T: _____
_____

F: _____
_____

A: _____
_____

R: _____
_____

Thought Download

Unintentional Model

C: _____
_____

T: _____
_____

F: _____
_____

A: _____
_____

R: _____
_____

Intentional Model

C: _____
_____

T: _____
_____

F: _____
_____

A: _____
_____

R: _____
_____

Thought Download

Unintentional Model	Intentional Model
C: _____	**C:** _____
T: _____	**T:** _____
F: _____	**F:** _____
A: _____	**A:** _____
R: _____	**R:** _____

Thought Download

Unintentional Model

C: _____
_____

T: _____
_____

F: _____
_____

A: _____
_____

R: _____
_____

Intentional Model

C: _____
_____

T: _____
_____

F: _____
_____

A: _____
_____

R: _____
_____

►Thought Download◄

Unintentional Model

C: _____
_____

T: _____
_____

F: _____
_____

A: _____
_____

R: _____
_____

Intentional Model

C: _____
_____

T: _____
_____

F: _____
_____

A: _____
_____

R: _____
_____

▶ Thought Download ◀

Unintentional Model

C: _____
_____

T: _____
_____

F: _____
_____

A: _____
_____

R: _____
_____

Intentional Model

C: _____
_____

T: _____
_____

F: _____
_____

A: _____
_____

R: _____
_____

► *Thought Download* ◄

Unintentional Model

C: _____
_____

T: _____
_____

F: _____
_____

A: _____
_____

R: _____
_____

Intentional Model

C: _____
_____

T: _____
_____

F: _____
_____

A: _____
_____

R: _____
_____

Date: _____

Thought Download

Unintentional Model

C: _____
_____

T: _____
_____

F: _____
_____

A: _____
_____

R: _____
_____

Intentional Model

C: _____
_____

T: _____
_____

F: _____
_____

A: _____
_____

R: _____
_____

___

Thought Download

Unintentional Model

C: _____
_____

T: _____
_____

F: _____
_____

A: _____
_____

R: _____
_____

Intentional Model

C: _____
_____

T: _____
_____

F: _____
_____

A: _____
_____

R: _____
_____

Thought Download

Unintentional Model

C: _____
_____

T: _____
_____

F: _____
_____

A: _____
_____

R: _____
_____

Intentional Model

C: _____
_____

T: _____
_____

F: _____
_____

A: _____
_____

R: _____
_____

Thought Download

Unintentional Model

C: _____
_____

T: _____
_____

F: _____
_____

A: _____
_____

R: _____
_____

Intentional Model

C: _____
_____

T: _____
_____

F: _____
_____

A: _____
_____

R: _____
_____

Thought Download

Unintentional Model

C: _____
_____

T: _____
_____

F: _____
_____

A: _____
_____

R: _____
_____

Intentional Model

C: _____
_____

T: _____
_____

F: _____
_____

A: _____
_____

R: _____
_____

Thought Download

Unintentional Model

C: _____
_____

T: _____
_____

F: _____
_____

A: _____
_____

R: _____
_____

Intentional Model

C: _____
_____

T: _____
_____

F: _____
_____

A: _____
_____

R: _____
_____

Thought Download

Unintentional Model

C: _____
_____

T: _____
_____

F: _____
_____

A: _____
_____

R: _____
_____

Intentional Model

C: _____
_____

T: _____
_____

F: _____
_____

A: _____
_____

R: _____
_____

Thought Download

Unintentional Model

C: _____

T: _____

F: _____

A: _____

R: _____

Intentional Model

C: _____

T: _____

F: _____

A: _____

R: _____

Thought Download

Unintentional Model

C: _____
_____

T: _____
_____

F: _____
_____

A: _____
_____

R: _____
_____

Intentional Model

C: _____
_____

T: _____
_____

F: _____
_____

A: _____
_____

R: _____
_____

Thought Download

Unintentional Model

C: _____

_____

T: _____

_____

F: _____

_____

A: _____

_____

R: _____

_____

Intentional Model

C: _____

_____

T: _____

_____

F: _____

_____

A: _____

_____

R: _____

_____

Thought Download

Unintentional Model	Intentional Model
C: _____	**C:** _____
T: _____	**T:** _____
F: _____	**F:** _____
A: _____	**A:** _____
R: _____	**R:** _____

▶ *Thought Download* ◀

Unintentional Model

C: _____
_____

T: _____
_____

F: _____
_____

A: _____
_____

R: _____
_____

Intentional Model

C: _____
_____

T: _____
_____

F: _____
_____

A: _____
_____

R: _____
_____

Thought Download

Unintentional Model

C: _____
_____

T: _____
_____

F: _____
_____

A: _____
_____

R: _____
_____

Intentional Model

C: _____
_____

T: _____
_____

F: _____
_____

A: _____
_____

R: _____
_____

Thought Download

Unintentional Model

C: _____
_____

T: _____
_____

F: _____
_____

A: _____
_____

R: _____
_____

Intentional Model

C: _____
_____

T: _____
_____

F: _____
_____

A: _____
_____

R: _____
_____

Thought Download

Unintentional Model	Intentional Model
C: _____	**C:** _____
_____	_____
T: _____	**T:** _____
_____	_____
F: _____	**F:** _____
_____	_____
A: _____	**A:** _____
_____	_____
R: _____	**R:** _____
_____	_____

Thought Download

Unintentional Model

C: _____
_____

T: _____
_____

F: _____
_____

A: _____
_____

R: _____
_____

Intentional Model

C: _____
_____

T: _____
_____

F: _____
_____

A: _____
_____

R: _____
_____

Thought Download

Unintentional Model

C: _____
_____

T: _____
_____

F: _____
_____

A: _____
_____

R: _____
_____

Intentional Model

C: _____
_____

T: _____
_____

F: _____
_____

A: _____
_____

R: _____
_____

Thought Download

Unintentional Model

C: _____
_____

T: _____
_____

F: _____
_____

A: _____
_____

R: _____
_____

Intentional Model

C: _____
_____

T: _____
_____

F: _____
_____

A: _____
_____

R: _____
_____

Thought Download

Unintentional Model

C: _____
_____

T: _____
_____

F: _____
_____

A: _____
_____

R: _____
_____

Intentional Model

C: _____
_____

T: _____
_____

F: _____
_____

A: _____
_____

R: _____
_____

Thought Download

Unintentional Model

C: _____
_____

T: _____
_____

F: _____
_____

A: _____
_____

R: _____
_____

Intentional Model

C: _____
_____

T: _____
_____

F: _____
_____

A: _____
_____

R: _____
_____

Thought Download

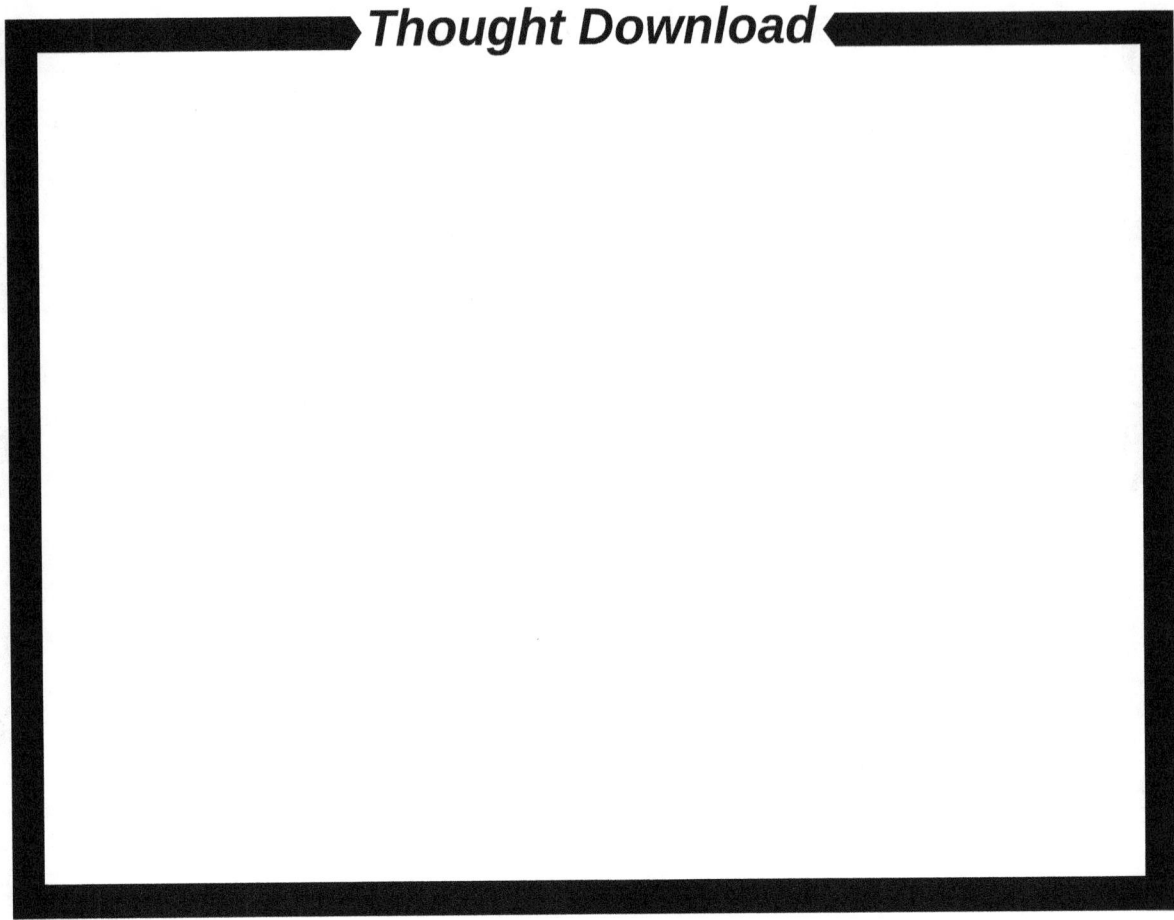

Unintentional Model

C: _____
_____

T: _____
_____

F: _____
_____

A: _____
_____

R: _____
_____

Intentional Model

C: _____
_____

T: _____
_____

F: _____
_____

A: _____
_____

R: _____
_____

Thought Download

Unintentional Model

C: _____

_____

T: _____

_____

F: _____

_____

A: _____

_____

R: _____

_____

Intentional Model

C: _____

_____

T: _____

_____

F: _____

_____

A: _____

_____

R: _____

_____

Thought Download

Unintentional Model

C: _____
_____

T: _____
_____

F: _____
_____

A: _____
_____

R: _____
_____

Intentional Model

C: _____
_____

T: _____
_____

F: _____
_____

A: _____
_____

R: _____
_____

Thought Download

Unintentional Model

C: _____
_____

T: _____
_____

F: _____
_____

A: _____
_____

R: _____
_____

Intentional Model

C: _____
_____

T: _____
_____

F: _____
_____

A: _____
_____

R: _____
_____

▶ *Thought Download* ◀

Unintentional Model

C: _____
_____

T: _____
_____

F: _____
_____

A: _____
_____

R: _____
_____

Intentional Model

C: _____
_____

T: _____
_____

F: _____
_____

A: _____
_____

R: _____
_____

Thought Download

Unintentional Model

C: _____
_____

T: _____
_____

F: _____
_____

A: _____
_____

R: _____
_____

Intentional Model

C: _____
_____

T: _____
_____

F: _____
_____

A: _____
_____

R: _____
_____

Thought Download

Unintentional Model

C: _____
_____

T: _____
_____

F: _____
_____

A: _____
_____

R: _____
_____

Intentional Model

C: _____
_____

T: _____
_____

F: _____
_____

A: _____
_____

R: _____
_____

Thought Download

Unintentional Model

C: _____
_____

T: _____
_____

F: _____
_____

A: _____
_____

R: _____
_____

Intentional Model

C: _____
_____

T: _____
_____

F: _____
_____

A: _____
_____

R: _____
_____

Thought Download

Unintentional Model

C: _____
_____

T: _____
_____

F: _____
_____

A: _____
_____

R: _____
_____

Intentional Model

C: _____
_____

T: _____
_____

F: _____
_____

A: _____
_____

R: _____
_____

►Thought Download◄

Unintentional Model

C: _____
_____

T: _____
_____

F: _____
_____

A: _____
_____

R: _____
_____

Intentional Model

C: _____
_____

T: _____
_____

F: _____
_____

A: _____
_____

R: _____
_____

Thought Download

Unintentional Model

C: _____
_____

T: _____
_____

F: _____
_____

A: _____
_____

R: _____

Intentional Model

C: _____
_____

T: _____
_____

F: _____
_____

A: _____
_____

R: _____
_____

Thought Download

Unintentional Model

C: _____
_____

T: _____
_____

F: _____
_____

A: _____
_____

R: _____
_____

Intentional Model

C: _____
_____

T: _____
_____

F: _____
_____

A: _____
_____

R: _____
_____

Thought Download

Unintentional Model

C: _____
_____

T: _____
_____

F: _____
_____

A: _____
_____

R: _____
_____

Intentional Model

C: _____
_____

T: _____
_____

F: _____
_____

A: _____
_____

R: _____
_____

Thought Download

Unintentional Model

C: _____
_____

T: _____
_____

F: _____
_____

A: _____
_____

R: _____
_____

Intentional Model

C: _____
_____

T: _____
_____

F: _____
_____

A: _____
_____

R: _____
_____

Thought Download

Unintentional Model

C: _____
_____

T: _____
_____

F: _____
_____

A: _____
_____

R: _____
_____

Intentional Model

C: _____
_____

T: _____
_____

F: _____
_____

A: _____
_____

R: _____
_____

►Thought Download◄

Unintentional Model

C: _____
_____

T: _____
_____

F: _____
_____

A: _____
_____

R: _____
_____

Intentional Model

C: _____
_____

T: _____
_____

F: _____
_____

A: _____
_____

R: _____
_____

Thought Download

Unintentional Model

C: _____
_____

T: _____
_____

F: _____
_____

A: _____
_____

R: _____
_____

Intentional Model

C: _____
_____

T: _____
_____

F: _____
_____

A: _____
_____

R: _____
_____

Thought Download

Unintentional Model

C: _____
_____

T: _____
_____

F: _____
_____

A: _____
_____

R: _____
_____

Intentional Model

C: _____
_____

T: _____
_____

F: _____
_____

A: _____
_____

R: _____
_____

Date: _____

Thought Download

Unintentional Model

C: _____
_____

T: _____
_____

F: _____
_____

A: _____
_____

R: _____
_____

Intentional Model

C: _____
_____

T: _____
_____

F: _____
_____

A: _____
_____

R: _____
_____

Thought Download

Unintentional Model

C: _____
_____

T: _____
_____

F: _____
_____

A: _____
_____

R: _____
_____

Intentional Model

C: _____
_____

T: _____
_____

F: _____
_____

A: _____
_____

R: _____
_____

Date: _____

Thought Download

Unintentional Model

C: _____
_____

T: _____
_____

F: _____
_____

A: _____
_____

R: _____
_____

Intentional Model

C: _____
_____

T: _____
_____

F: _____
_____

A: _____
_____

R: _____
_____

Thought Download

Unintentional Model

C: _____
_____

T: _____
_____

F: _____
_____

A: _____
_____

R: _____
_____

Intentional Model

C: _____
_____

T: _____
_____

F: _____
_____

A: _____
_____

R: _____
_____

Thought Download

Unintentional Model

C: _____
_____

T: _____
_____

F: _____
_____

A: _____
_____

R: _____
_____

Intentional Model

C: _____
_____

T: _____
_____

F: _____
_____

A: _____
_____

R: _____
_____

Thought Download

Unintentional Model

C: _____
_____

T: _____
_____

F: _____
_____

A: _____
_____

R: _____
_____

Intentional Model

C: _____
_____

T: _____
_____

F: _____
_____

A: _____
_____

R: _____
_____

_____

Thought Download

Unintentional Model

C: _____
_____

T: _____
_____

F: _____
_____

A: _____
_____

R: _____
_____

Intentional Model

C: _____
_____

T: _____
_____

F: _____
_____

A: _____
_____

R: _____
_____

Inspiration

Inspiration

Inspiration

Inspiration

Inspiration

Inspiration

Inspiration

Inspiration

Inspiration

Inspiration

Inspiration

Inspiration

Inspiration

Inspiration

Inspiration

Inspiration

Inspiration

Inspiration

Inspiration

Inspiration

Inspiration

Inspiration

Inspiration

Inspiration

Inspiration

Amy Twiggs #1 Best Selling Author.
She is a wife and a mother of four teenagers.
She is a former elite gymnast and in 1993 she was a member of the National Women's Gymnastics Team. She received a full-ride athletic scholarship for gymnastics from Stanford University where she obtained a Bachelor's Degree in Psychology with a focus in Health & Development. She is professionally certified through The Life Coach School in mental & emotional health tools that greatly enhance clients overall performance and life experience. Mental Strength Training & Confidence Coaching is her passion. Amy's education has provided many opportunities for her to give back to athletes and coaches. She currently lives in St. George, Utah.
You can contact Amy at:
FlippinAwesomeCoaching.com

www.ingramcontent.com/pod-product-compliance
Lightning Source LLC
Chambersburg PA
CBHW081250040426

42452CB00015B/2776